This book is dedicated to all the people who are living covenant relationships and are committed to showing this broken world the healing power of love.

And we would like to personally thank:

Earl & Darliene Johnson, Gene & Nell Nicolet and Bill & Beni Johnson for showing Sheri and I the power of generational blessing and inheritance. Our family has been transformed in one generation because of your example of love and commitment.

LovingOnPurpose.com
© Copyright 2008

"I think it is time to take our relationship to the next level! Do you know what that means?"

"Yes... ...we are going to have the infamous "DTR Talk""

"*It is amazing how universal Danny's materials are. I supervise a team of twelve individuals from age 23-55 yrs from various cultures and value systems. I find myself quoting "Dannyisms" to them all the time. He makes me look so smart!*"

Sadie

"*When Danny has taught on relationships to our staff, he has consistently been the speaker who our employees want back the most.*"

Eric

Contents

Message from Danny pg.8

Lessons

1. Introduction pg.11
2. D-Day pg.23
3. A Commited Life pg.33
4. 7 Pillars of a Healthy Relationship pg.43
5. 5 Love Languages pg.53
6. Your Normal pg.65
7. Communication Dance pg.75
8. Conflict Resolution pg.93
9. 90/10 Connection pg.103

Appendix pg.117

Thank you for joining me as I lead you around this relationship of yours. I hope you learn something. My wife, Sheri, and I have learned most of what we know about relationships from our own marriage. In 1984, we entered a journey neither of us was ready for. It is difficult to be prepared for the unknown, but it was even more difficult for us to prepare for what was coming. Marriage would require both Sheri and I to completely change the way we had ever lived life, or for that matter, ever seen it lived. The two of us were going to take 15 years (Sheri says it was only 12) trying to hang on to our family while we were molded into totally different people. Many times it did not look like we were going to make it. But thanks be to Jesus, through many tears, fights, and disconnects we forged a union that, today; we will both die to protect.

Romance and the hope of being loved by someone are intoxicating. Many times, we unwittingly pull "God's will" into our desires to be with someone and end up plowing through the red flags, parental and leader input and create a situation God never intended for our lives. The term I use for this dynamic is "Laa-La-la." It makes everything better than it really is and helps me to minimize issues that build destructively into our relationship. "La-laa-la" can help me walk right into a poor decision.

Whether you are in a pre-engagement situation or have decided to move ahead toward marriage, this series will present you with perspectives that only someone who has lived it can give you. I've stripped the Laa-la-la off as best I can and want you to think, maybe for the first time, about some important qualities about your relationship. I hope to impart to you wisdom and understanding that empowers you both. The power that you will both need comes from courage, the kind of courage that only truth brings us. When God speaks truth to our hearts it ignites a courage that would lead us to face our greatest fears. Sometimes this fear is rejection and sometimes it's commitment. Either way, the Defining the Relationship series will allow you a rare opportunity to look that fear in the eye and make a grace-filled decision one way or the other. God bless you in this courageous adventure!

Danny Silk

"What this course did for us was amazing! Danny didn't give us the secret to a relationship without issues or problems.(There isn't one) What he gave us were the tools needed in order to deal with everyday life together. The tools Danny imparted to us have stayed with us throughout the ups and downs of our marriage, and have allowed for us to build and re-build our relationship into what we had both hoped for when this whole journey started."

Aaron

Defining The Relationship
RELATIONSHIP SKILLS SERIES

1 Introduction
Goals, Outline and Expectations

Class Topics
- Group Activity
- For Whom
- Goals
- Outline
- Recap
- Couple Activity
- About Next Week

For Whom
- A premarital course for those considering or preparing for marriage.

Goals

Couple Goals
- Find out how close to this person you should get and whether you should marry them.
- Write in the notes column any additional goals you, as a couple may have for this course.

Group Activity
- Introduce yourself to another couple.
- Be prepared to introduce them to the group.

Notes

Defining The Relationship

1 Introduction

Notes

Instructor's Goals:
- To give you the **courage** to make a **decision** to move ahead or a **decision** to stop and walk away.
- To help you look at the decision you are about to make.
- To teach you things about yourself, relationships, and life.
- To teach you about the value of having **purpose** and a mission in your relationship.

> Hey, I'm ready to go! Look I got a tux and everything! I don't really need this! I,m going to marry you no matter what I learn here.

What is she thinking?

LovingOnPurpose.com
© Copyright 2008

Page: 12
Written by: Danny Silk

RELATIONSHIP SKILLS SERIES

Goals, Outline and Expectations

Outline:

Class 1:
Introduction
- An introduction to *Defining the Relationship*
- A Lesson that covers the Goals, Outlines and Expectations.

Class 2:
D-Day
- One of the most important things you can learn as a couple is how to knit your **hearts** together and not to just simply **get along**.
- Learn the value of becoming *powerful*.

I wonder if I am ready for this kind of commitment?

Defining The Relationship

1 Introduction

Notes

Class 3:
A Committed Life - Loving on Purpose
- Discover the value of creating an *intimate connection*.
- Learn about covenant relationship and how to *intentionally* love the other person.

Class 4:
The 7 Pillars of a Healthy Relationship
- Create value for:
  - **Respect**
  - Love
  - **Self Control**
  - Personal Responsibility
  - Truth, Trust and Trustworthiness
  - Vision
  - Faith

RELATIONSHIP SKILLS SERIES

Goals, Outline and Expectations

Notes

Class 5:
The 5 Love Languages

- The greatest service that you have to offer is the service of **sacrificial** love.
- Discover the goal of love, the **source** of love and how we each experience love.

> I wish we could just get married and be together. He's so perfect.

Defining The Relationship

1 Introduction

Notes

Class 6:
Your "Normal"
- Understand what we bring as "normal" to this relationship and why we bring it!

Class 7:
The Communication Dance
- We should each spend a great deal of time learning to communicate.
- Learn how to hear the needs each of you have and quit trying to convince each other to agree on the same thing.
- Tell them about you, not about them.
- Take a look at how to cultivate **respect** through the communication processes.
- Protect the priority of the heart to heart **connection** while we work to resolve our differences.

RELATIONSHIP SKILLS SERIES

Goals, Outline and Expectations

Notes

Class 8:
Resolving Conflict
- Learn the difference between **listening** and **speaking**.
- Take a look at the different listening skills available while communicating.
- Learn how to reduce the anxiety caused by disagreements and protect the connection with love.

Class 9:
The 90/10 Connection
- What is intimacy if it is not sex?
- What are the differences between men and women.
- Learn how to create a place where intimacy can flourish and not be injured.

I thought we never argue! What is happening?

LovingOnPurpose.com
© Copyright 2008
Written by: Danny Silk

Defining The Relationship

1 Introduction

Recap

Instructors Goals:
- To give you the _____ to make a _____ to move ahead or a _____ to stop and walk away.
- To teach you about the value of having _____ and a mission in your relationship.

Class 2:
D-Day
- One of the most important things you can learn as a couple is how to knit your _____ together and not to just simply _____.
- Learn the value of becoming _____.

Class 3:
A Committed Life - Loving on Purpose
- Discovering the value of creating an _____.
- Learn about covenant relationship and how to _____ love the other person.

Class 4:
The 7 Pillars of a Healthy Relationship
- Create value for:
   - _____

Goals, Outline and Expectations

- Love
- _____
- Personal Responsibility
- Truth, Trust and Trustworthiness
- Vision
- Faith

Class 5:
The 5 Love Languages
- The greatest service that you have to offer is the service of _____ love.
- Discover the goal of love, the _____ of love and how we each experience love.

Class 7:
The Communication Dance
- Take a look at how to cultivate _____ through the communication processes.
- Protect the priority of the heart to heart _____ while we work to resolve our differences.

Class 8:
Resolving Conflict
- Learn the difference between _____ _____ and _____.

Defining The Relationship

1 Introduction

Couple Activity

Write down why you are getting married and why you chose this person.

Compare your answers now with how you feel at the end of the course.

Names: _____
_____
Last Name _____
Location: _____
Date: _____

_____
_____
_____
_____
_____
_____
_____
_____
_____
_____
_____
_____
_____
_____

RELATIONSHIP SKILLS SERIES

Goals, Outline and Expectations

"Throughout the class, I can confidently say that Danny's teaching gives obtainable life advice (skills to be learned) and tools that allow both a husband and a wife to want to work through situations that may arise in marriage. Furthermore, the class makes couples begin to ask the hard questions about "Is this what we should or want to be doing." Because asking yourself the questions is better than having everyone elses opinions.

I believe the class empowers you and your spouse/fiance/girlfriend/boyfriend to want to answer the hard questions."

Rebekkah

Defining The Relationship
RELATIONSHIP SKILLS SERIES

2 D-Day
Decisions are the Doorway to Responsibility

Class Topics
- Introduction
- Powerful vs. Powerless
- Levi's Story
- Recap

Introduction
- Do you understand the power you must exercise to make this decision?
- Do you understand what you are about to create?
- Our decisions can remove family *history* curses and plant eternal *blessings* for our descendents and legacy.

Points to Ponder
- Decisions are the doorway to *responsibility*.
- God loves you more than He loves your marriage and more than He hates divorce.
- Do you understand the power you need in order to make this decision?

Defining The Relationship

2 D-Day

Notes

- You are not just improving the quality of <u>your</u> life by getting married, you are improving the life of the generations to come.
- The Gospel of *Power* flows through *powerful* people by the decisions they make.
- God hates *broken* covenants because of what they do to the flow of blessings to following generations — the innocent *recipients* of your *decisions*.

Decisions are the Doorway to Responsibility

- This is how God works:

> "You did not choose Me, but I chose you and appointed you that you should go and bear fruit, and that your fruit should remain, that whatever you ask the Father in My name He may give you." John 15:16

- No one comes to Him unless He calls them. That is powerful!!!
- I am in this relationship because I **chose** you! Don't ever forget that.
- I take full responsibility for my choice towards you for the rest of my life.
- I chose you out of a **decision** to **love** you.

- Powerless + Powerless = Controlling
- Powerful + Powerless = Dependent
- Powerful + Powerful = Freedom

Defining The Relationship

2 D-Day

Notes

Powerless People

- Powerless people live *scared* and want *control*.
- Powerless people are famous for blaming the quality of their lives on someone else.
- Powerless people require others to *"make"* them happy and carry no personal *responsibility* toward meeting their own needs for peace and joy.

Powerful People

- Powerful people create *responsible* and *respectful*, *healthy* relationships.
- Powerful people are "happening" - responding to life, rather than reacting to it.
- Powerful people can *set limits* with people who are *abusive* and not have to change *who they are* to feel safe.

RELATIONSHIP SKILLS SERIES

Decisions are the Doorway to Responsibility

- Powerful people can direct the choices and decisions of their lives.
- Powerful people *manage* themselves *no matter* what others are doing.
- Powerful people take full responsibility for the quality of life they are creating and therefore living in.

Notes

I commit my strength to this relationship!

Defining The Relationship

2 D-Day

Notes

Our son, Levi's story

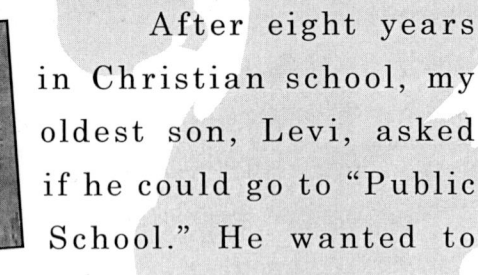

After eight years in Christian school, my oldest son, Levi, asked if he could go to "Public School." He wanted to play football and the local Christian High Schools didn't have a program. Sheri and I thought about it for a few fear-filled moments and asked him a question that only a powerful person could answer. I asked, "Levi, we are afraid of what might happen to you, us and our family if we let you go into that environment. Why would your mother and I be really smart to say 'yes' to public school?"

He knew this was his big moment. Everything is depending on his answer. What is he going to say? He first lowered his eyes and then shot a look into my eyes. And then it came, an answer I didn't expect. He said, "Why should you

Decisions are the Doorway to Responsibility

feel smart about letting me go to public high school? Because I will not break your hearts."

Dumbfounded, we stood there looking at him. I then grinned, showing how proud I was of him. I was so scared and happy at the same time. Levi gets it! He gets that it is his job to carry his side of our relationship. It's not our job to keep him out of trouble. It is his job to protect our relationship with the way he makes his decisions in a place with so many bad choices. He graduated from a public high school. And, he was right. He did not break our hearts. A powerful young man directed himself to demonstrate love and honor in the decisions he made. Only powerful people can build loving relationships.

Defining The Relationship

2 D-Day

Recap

Introduction
- Our decisions can remove family _____ curses and plant eternal _____ for our descendents and legacy.
- The Gospel of _____ flows through _____ people.
- God hates _____ covenants because of what they do to the flow of blessings to following generations – the innocent _____ of your _____.
- This is how God works:
  - I chose you out of a _____ to _____ you.

Powerless People
- Powerless people live _____ and want _____.
- Powerless people require others to "_____" them happy and carry no personal _____ toward meeting their own needs for peace and joy.

Powerful People
- Powerful people create _____ and _____, _____ relationships
-

RELATIONSHIP SKILLS SERIES

Decisions are the Doorway to Responsibility

- Powerful people can _____ with people who are _____ and not have to change _____ to feel safe.
- Powerful people _____ themselves _____ what others are doing.

"Recently a friend asked me to advise him in his relationship. They were having some struggles and needed some direction. As I spoke with him I realized that Danny's words were coming out of my mouth. My friend's eyes lit up as he began to get hope for their relationship.

Even though I really felt like the things I said were from the very heart of God, I relized that it came from studying Danny's DTR book. I thank the Lord for tools like this that are not only applicable for anyone involved in a relationship, but also for ministering to couples."

Graeme

Defining The Relationship
Relationship Skills Series

3 The Committed Life
Loving On Purpose

Class Topics
- Destiny, Vision and Purpose
- Mission Statements
- Recap

Objectives

Discover your Destiny, Vision and Purpose

Create a Mission Statement for yourselves and your Marriage

Destiny, Vision and Purpose

Dang you look hot at 73 baby!

Notes

- Destiny is the **Road** we are on.
- "Describe the "good life" that you lived as if you are sitting on the front porch at age 80 together"

Defining The Relationship

3 The Committed Life

Notes

- What will the journey to that destination look like?
- Have you thought of that destination?
- Make sure your *marriage* doesn't outlast your *destination*.

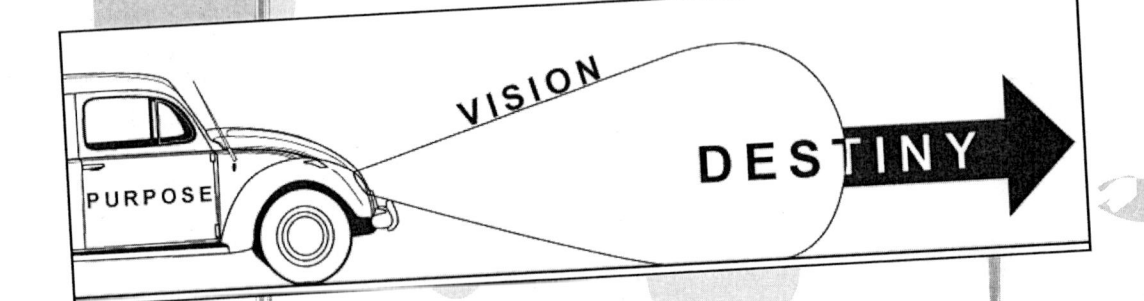

- Vision is the **head lights** helping to reveal our *destiny*.
- People were built to **hope**. Vision creates **hope** for your *destiny*.

"A Man without a *Vision*, is a Man without a Future. And a man without a Future, will always return to the *Past*."

Loving On Purpose

Notes

- If you are not looking down the road at your future, then you will long for the glory of the old days. Without a vision of your destination the best will be behind you.
- Purpose or Mission is the vehicle that **drives** us towards our **destiny.**
  - You must be intentional with your purpose to reach your destiny!
  - The purpose or mission keeps us from being detoured from the road to our destiny.

Defining the Relationship

3 The Committed Life

Verbs

advance	strive
exist	choose
meet	gaze
search	repair
advise	study
expect	clean
motivate	give
see	promise
allow	succeed
explain	command
send	have
arrange	quake
express	sway
offer	complete
serve	heal
ask	read
facilitate	talk
open	confound
shake	hear
beg	rebuild
feel	taste
order	confront
shoot	help
believe	receive
find	teach
pay	connect
smile	hire
breathe	reconcile
finish	tell
permit	console
spend	hope
bring	recover
fix	think
persuade	create
stand	instruct
build	redeem
fly	translate
plan	cut
start	invite
buy	refuse
follow	travel
play	dance
stay	kneel
carry	release
forbid	try
point	dare
stimulate	lead
challenge	remember
force	understand
pray	decide
stop	learn
change	remove
free	use
preach	deliver

Your Mission Statement

Couple Task

The Goal:
- Define a purpose or a mission statement for your relationship:
  - What vision do you have for your destiny?
  - What is God's purpose for your relationship?

Verbs
1. Choose 10 of the verbs, from the Notes column, that best describes your relationship and write them in the page on the right.

Services
1. Choose 5 of the services, from the Notes column, that best describe how your relationship would serve others and write them in the page on the right.

RELATIONSHIP SKILLS SERIES

Loving On Purpose

Verbs cont.

leave	love
render	run
wait	write
direct	encourage
let	make
require	say
want	examine
discover	Add your own...
like	
restore	
warn	
draw	
listen	
reveal	
wish	
dream	
live	
revive	
work	
empower	

Services

Administering	Education
Organizing	Teaching
Aiding	Entertain
Planning	Transportge-lism
Art	Working
Politics	Excellence
Building	Worship
Prayer	Exhortation
Business	Writing
Prophecy	Feeding
Cleaning	Love
Reading	Giving
Comforting	Massage
Revival	Harvest
Cooking	Medicine
Running	Healing
Counsel	Mercy
Salvation	Health
Dancing	Music
Serving	Hospitality
Deliverance	Leading
Sewing	Intercession
Dental	Add your own...
Singing	
Economics	
Supporter	

Written by: Danny Silk

Defining the Relationship

3 The Committed Life

Notes

Target

1. Choose 3 of the targets, from the list below, that best describe what you are pointing your lives at. Then write them below:

_____
_____
_____
_____

Targets

Africa	social-services	single
America	social-systems	relationships
Asia	economic-system	men
South America	lost	women
Europe	pre-believers	married
Australia	saved	children
New Zealand	searching	poor
Canada	possessed	church
Asians	abused	mission-field
Blacks	lonely	artists
Hispanics	sick	science
First-Nations-people	needy	athletes
all-peoples	neglected	musicians
legal-system	broken	entrepreneurs
medical-system	oppressed	business
political-system	terminally-ill	world
religious-system	under-privileged	cities
eternity-systems	wealthy	criminals
family-systems	hungry	violent-offenders
civil-systems	hurting	Earth
education-system	wounded	Heaven
	illiterate	Add your own...
	weak	
	divorced	

RELATIONSHIP SKILLS SERIES

Loving On Purpose

Notes

Assembly
- So you should have 10 verbs, 5 services and 3 targets.
- Reduce the verbs to 3, the services to 2 and the targets to the 1 that best describes the potential of your relationship.

Our Verbs
_____
_____
_____

Our Services
_____
_____

Our Target
_____

- Now fill out the form below to create a mission statement for your relationship:

Our Mission Statement

Date: _____

"**Our** mission in life is to ___*Verb 1*___, ___*Verb 2*___ and ___*Verb 3*___, (*in/with/to the) ___*Target*___ through ___*Service 1*___ and ___*Service 2*___!"

* Insert the appropriate words to connect the sentance.

Defining The Relationship

3 The Committed Life

Recap
- You want to make sure your _____ doesn't outlast your _____ .
- Vision is the _____ helping to reveal our _____ .
- People were built to _____ . Vision creates _____ for your _____ .
- Purpose or Mission is the thing that _____ us towards our _____ .

RELATIONSHIP SKILLS SERIES

Loving On Purpose

"C`mon help me with the answers so we can get done faster!"

LovingOnPurpose.com
© Copyright 2008

Page: 41
Written by: Danny Silk

"We are so grateful for the tools you have shared in these messages. After listening to the CDs, I realized I really don't even KNOW what a healthy marriage looks like! Neither of our sets of parents had one.

We just downloaded (7 Pillars of a Healthy Relationship) a couple days ago, and wow, it is like food to a weary traveler! We are 28 years from being "pre-marrieds", but it is not too late to learn what I wished we knew then!

So, Danny and Sheri, thank you!!! I think God is going to rejuvenate our lives and marriage, and you have been very key in that!"

Jill

Defining The Relationship
RELATIONSHIP SKILLS SERIES

4 7 Pillars of a Healthy Relationship

Class Topics
- Introduction
- 7 Pillars
- Recap

Proverbs 9:11
Wisdom has built her house, she has hewn out her 7 pillars...

Notes

Introduction
- The 7 pillars are the frame or *structure* you are creating to protect the *intimacy* in your marriage.

"Companionship... loyalty... support..."

DEFINING THE RELATIONSHIP

4 7 Healthy Relationship Pillars

Notes

Your gifts can not be cultivated apart from producing fruit or character in your life. We need both **gifts** and **character** to carry the glory of the Lord in our community and our families. This is how we partner with God to see His glory poured out on the earth. With our **gift** we demonstrate heaven.

With our **character** we validate heaven.

- Only healthy people can be happy.
- Lovers change to protect the love.
- The foundation of a healthy relationship is Unconditional Acceptance.
- The 7 Pillars hold up the peace, hope and joy of our covenant relationships.

RELATIONSHIP SKILLS SERIES

Proverbs 9:1

Notes

The 7 Pillars

1. Love
   - The outcome or quality of your environment.
   - A safe place for intimacy.
   - A safe place where you can be known by the other person.
   - Unconditional *acceptance* communicates that you get to be you and I get to be me.

I wonder if we have all 7 pillars in our relationship?

LovingOnPurpose.com
© Copyright 2008

Page: 45
Written by: Danny Silk

Defining The Relationship

4 7 Healthy Relationship Pillars

Notes

2. Honor
   - The result of **honor** is that you feel **powerful** around me.
   - I value you, listen, and engage with you.
   - Love and honor need to coexist. If you remove one, you threaten the other.

3. Self Control
   - I **manage** me no matter what you are doing or not doing.
   - I will manage myself toward protecting these pillars in my relationships.
   - I expect you to do the same.
   - I will never **blame** you for how I treat you.
   - If I have no control over me, I will not experience the freedom that Jesus died to give me.

> Proverbs 25:28
>
> Whoever has no rule over his own spirit is like a city broken down, without walls.

Proverbs 9:1

Notes

4. Responsibility
  - I must *respond* to the situations in my life, anticipate life and be prepared for it.
  - I need a plan for what I am going to do no matter what you choose to do.
  - Being able to *respond* is being Response-able.

Defining the Relationship

4 7 Pillars of a healthy relationship

Notes

5. Truth
- Truth, Trust & Trustworthiness are all forms of the same quality.

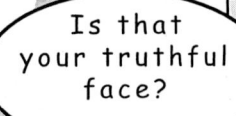

Is that your truthful face?

- I will courageously show you who I am even when I am afraid.
- Truth sets us free, free to be **ourselves** around each other
- I can handle who you are and I need you to be able to deal with who I am even though we are very different.
- Relationships are tested for trust through **conflict** and covenant.
- The lack of trust says more about you than it does the person you don't trust.

Proverbs 9:1

- There is no way someone can supply you with what you need if you do not tell them the truth.

6. Faith
   - We must have a supernatural supply of love and forgiveness.
   - My life must have a "boss" bigger than my best, most rational decision.
   - I must have a **supernatural** option as an outcome in my relationships. It cannot all be up to my best *efforts* and me.
   - God is my *supply* and you are my *target*!

7. Vision
   - Any relationship has to have a purpose.
   - Our *pain* needs a purpose.
   - The clarity of the vision allows me to rise above the *struggle* as a temporary situation instead of something *overwhelming*.

Defining the Relationship

4 7 Pillars of a healthy relationship

Recap
- The 7 pillars are the _____ you are creating to protect the _____ in your marriage.
- We need both _____ and _____ to carry the glory of the Lord in our community and our families.
- With our _____ we demonstrate heaven.
- With our _____ we validate heaven.

1. Love
- Unconditional _____ communicates that you get to be you and I get to be me.

2. Honor
- The result of _____ is that you feel _____ around me.

3. Self Control
- I _____ me no matter what you are doing or not doing.
- I will never _____ you for how I treat you.

4. Responsibility
- I must _____ to the situations in my life, anticipate life and be prepared for it.

Proverbs 9:1

- Being able to _____ is being Response-able.

5. Truth
    - Truth sets us free, free to be _____ around each other.
    - Relationships are tested for trust through _____ and covenant.

6. Faith
    - I must have a _____ option as an outcome in my relationships. It cannot all be up to my best _____ and me.
    - God is my _____ and you are my _____!

7. Vision
    - The clarity of the vision allows me to rise above the _____ as a temporary situation instead of something _____.

"*Ok this series rocks not only because you learn your love language which you can apply to all types of relationships but, also because Danny actually teaches from his own personal experience which adds value and strength to the series. I used one of the methods of communicating with my roommate and it worked marvelously...*"

Ingrid

"*When we heard Danny's teaching on the five Love Languages it helped our relationship so much. If I make sure to clear a path in the entry way before he gets home, and he is sure to give me a quick kiss and ask about my day, we are off to a fabulous night!*"

Angela

Defining The Relationship
Relationship Skills Series

5 5 Love Languages
The Intimate Connection

A book by Dr... Gary Chapman
www.fivelovelanguages.com

Class Topics
- Intimate Connections
- 5 Love Languages
- Recap

Intimate Connections

Relationships are kept healthy by:
- Creating a safe place by *protecting* the connection of that relationship.
- *Feeding* these connections with what they need.
- Making the connection a *priority*.
- Once we have a connection we learn to manage the strength of that connection.
- Disconnection fills our relationship with anxiety - the enemy of love.

The Connection

The goal of marriage should be to create a loving, intimate connection.

We have to believe that love is worth dying for. Jn 15:13

Notes

LovingOnPurpose.com
© Copyright 2008
Page: 53
Written by: Danny Silk

Defining The Relationship

5 5 Love Languages

Notes

- Communication is 100% more difficult in a disconnected state.
- Make connection the top priority before trying to work through a conflict or disagreement.

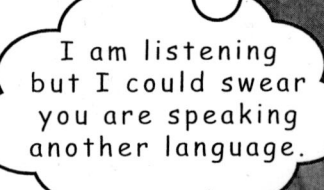

I am listening but I could swear you are speaking another language.

- Never allow "I love you very much" to be a secret from each other ... NEVER!
- Remember: People tend to speak "I love you" in their native language.
- I make a deep commitment to learn your language so you will know & experience my love for you.

RELATIONSHIP SKILLS SERIES

The Intimate Connection

Notes

5 Love Languages
- People are built to experience love.
- When they constantly don't feel loved, they will seek a safe place where they can protect themselves.

To Begin
- Be sure to learn your own love language so you can communicate what you will need from your partner.
- Learning their love language will help them trust that you care about them.
- Be sure to communicate back and forth what you discover about yourselves in this chapter.

Defining the Relationship

5 5 Love Languages

Notes

Gifts
- Do you feel especially loved when someone brings you gifts and other tangible expressions of love?
- Connection
  - "You *know* me and were *thinking* of me when you were out."

"Wow, I had no idea that gifts meant so much to you!"

- Disconnection
  - "You don't care because you don't even know me or give me a passing thought."

The Intimate Connection

Touch
- Do you feel especially loved when someone expresses feelings through physical contact?
- Connection
  - "I feel loved when we are *touching*."
- Disconnection
  - "I feel rejected and neglected when you don't touch me!"

Defining The Relationship

5 5 Love Languages

Notes

Acts of Service
- Do you feel especially loved when someone pitched in to help you, perhaps by running errands or taking on your household chores?
- Connection
  - "I feel loved when you *take care* of the things that are important to me!"

You're really sexy when you do dishes!

The Intimate Connection

Notes

- Disconnection
  - "You don't care about me, because you don't care about the things that are important to me."

Quality Time
- Do you feel especially loved when someone gives you their undivided attention?
- Connection
  - "I feel loved when you show *interest* in me."

When you said, "Let's go camping!" I had no idea this is what you had in mind.

- Disconnection
  - "I feel hurt and invalidated when you don't have time for me or cannot pay attention in our conversations."

Defining The Relationship

5 Love Languages

Notes

Words of Affirmation
- Do you feel especially loved when people express how grateful they are for you, and for the simple, everyday things you do?
- Connection
  - "I feel loved when you *like* me, *enjoy* me and *believe* in me."

- Disconnection
  - "I feel rejected when your words are harsh."

Questions from the lovelanguage.com 30sec survey:
http://www.fivelovelanguages.com/30sec.html#love

RELATIONSHIP SKILLS SERIES

The Intimate Connection

Notes

In Closing

- Now, take time to discuss the two love languages that best describe you. When you take the time to learn another person's love language then you will effectively get your message across the **communication** bridge into their hearts.
- You will immediately see the effect, as they *light up* and are *nourished*.

Defining the Relationship

5 5 Love Languages

Recap

Intimate Connections
- Relationships are kept healthy by:
  - Creating a safe place by _____ the relationship connections.
  - _____ these connections with what they need.
  - Making the connection a _____.

Gifts
- Connection
  - "You _____ me and were _____ of me when you were out."

Touch
- Connection
  - "I feel loved when we are _____."

Acts of Service
- Connection
  - "I feel loved when you _____ of the things that are important to me!"

Quality Time
- Connection
  - "I feel loved when you show _____ in me."

The Intimate Connection

Words of Affirmation
- Connection
  - "I feel loved when you _____ me, _____ me and _____ in me."

In Closing
- Now, take time to discuss the two love languages that best describe you. When you take the time to learn another person's love language then you will effectively get your message across the _____ bridge into their hearts.
- You will immediately see the effect, as they _____ and are _____.

"When my husband and I first started listening to Danny's messages on relationships, specifically on marriage and connection, we realized we had been disconnected for 80% of our marriage.

Our normal was to be disconnected and Danny challenged that. He challenged us to have a "new normal". He taught us how to protect connection with each other and with our kids, and how to value it. He taught us how to get connected as a family, and stay connected. We are so grateful for the tools Danny gave us. It has forever changed us for the better."

Nicole

6 Your Normal

Class Topics
- Introduction
- Family History
- Curses and Blessings
- Power
- Recap

Introduction
- The "sins of the fathers" are the *templates* of our family "*normal*" that are past on from generation to generation.
- They are formed through the *agreements* that we make about what is true.
- Our families create our "*normal*" like factories for children who cannot filter out what is not true or harmful to the way relationships flourish.

What are you bringing?

The Power
You have the power to cut down and out all the decisions that don't bear good fruit in your life.

Num 14:18
"The LORD is slow to anger and abundant in lovingkindness, forgiving iniquity and transgression; but He will by no means clear the guilty, visiting the iniquity of the fathers on the children to the third and the fourth generations.'"

Defining The Relationship

6 Your Normal

Notes

Family History

- The sins of the fathers will be visited on the children's, children's, children.
- The sins of the fathers is not just limited to a curse or spiritual open door, but it includes **agreements** in the spirit realm.
- Spiritual assignments are made through **agreement**, charging your home with whatever you agree with.
- This forms part of our family "*normal*".

You had me at "yachtakk ta kakyached!

RELATIONSHIP SKILLS SERIES

What are you bringing?

Notes

Curses and Blessings

- Understanding what I've learned as "normal" helps me own my family history and what I'll be bringing into this relationship.
- The person I am with will feel my family history *momentum*, either good or destructive.
- Previous to this class, we may not be aware of what it was that we were feeling, but now we know that we are having a clash of "normals".
- Talking about the way these paradigms developed in our lives will help both of us realize what we are feeling.
- Together we can *decide* what stays and what goes. This is more difficult than you might think, but the process starts with *discovery*.

Defining The Relationship

6 Your Normal

Notes

> Lk 3:9
>
> "Indeed the axe is already laid at the root of the trees; so every tree that does not bear good fruit is cut down and thrown into the fire."

Power

- You have the power to chop down every tree that doesn't bear good fruit.
- You have the power to create a normal that is full of *blessing* and not *curses*.
- You get to create an entirely different "normal" for your children.
- It is not OK to just react the opposite way, because that usually has the same root of fear.
- What has to change is what you *agreed* with.
- Partnering with *fear*, let those curses into your family's life and therefore you must let *love* rule where *fear* ruled before.

RELATIONSHIP SKILLS SERIES

What are you bringing?

Notes

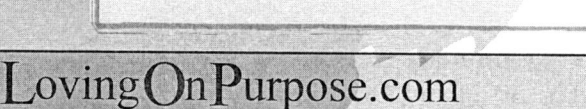

- Perfect *love* casts out all fear!
- The goal is to eliminate *fear*, to stop the curse flowing to the next generation.
- You must learn how to trust and how to be intimate, open and honest.
- You are going to have to learn how to create high levels of respect.

Romans 12:2

"And do not be conformed to this world, but be transformed by the renewing of your mind, so that you may prove what the will of God is, that which is good and acceptable and perfect."

- Through the power of a *transformed mind*, we can create a *new "normal"*. We are transformed by the renewing of our minds.

Hey... Danny didn't say "trade" my mind for yours!

Defining The Relationship

6 Your Normal

Notes

What is "Normal"?
- The two of you will combine your "normals" to create a new one for your family.
- Simply pledging to "Never do what my parents did" will not break the **paradigm** from passing into your family.
- Fear or resentment must go. These are negative ways to attract inheritance from our family history.
- Change comes through **new agreements** with truth. We will first need to find lies that are buried in our "normal" and break our **agreements** with these lies.
- Building love in our families starts with confronting the **fears** that have remained in them and learning new ways to apply truth.
- Our primary objectives are to learn to build trust, intimacy and connection and to eliminate all the lies that

RELATIONSHIP SKILLS SERIES

What are you bringing?

keep us unsuccessful in these areas.

- We create a new family "normal" through the power of a transformed mind.

Notes

> Hey, you're pretty cute on the outside! What do you look like on the inside?

Defining the Relationship

6 Your Normal

Recap
- The "sins of the fathers" are the _____ of our family *"normal"* that are passed on from generation to generation.
- They are formed through the _____ that we make about what is true.

Family History
- The sins of the fathers are not just limited to a curse or spiritual open door, but include _____ in the spirit realm.
- Spiritual assignments are made through _____, charging your home with what ever you agree with.

Curses and Blessings
- The person I am with will feel my family history _____, either good or destructive.
- Together we can _____ what stays and what goes. This is more difficult than you might think, but the process starts with _____.

Power
- You have the power to create a "normal" that is full of _____ and not _____.

RELATIONSHIP SKILLS SERIES

Goals, Outline and Expectations

- What has to change is what you _____ with.
- Partnering with _____, let those curses into your family's life and therefore you must let _____ rule where _____ ruled before.
- Perfect _____ casts out all fear!
- The goal is to eliminate _____, to stop the curse flowing to the next generation.
- Through the power of a _____ we can create a _____. We are transformed by the renewing of our minds.

What is "Normal"?

- Simply pledging to "Never do what my parents did" will not break the _____ from passing into your family.
- Change comes through _____ with truth. We will first need to find lies that are buried in our "normal" and break our _____ with these lies.
- Building love in our families starts with confronting the _____ that have remained in them and learning new ways to apply truth.

"Well before the class we didn't really understand the communication styles - that you can be passive with one person and passive-aggresive with another, just depending on the relationship.

We don't have conflicts often but when we do, it isn't pretty. So hearing how to work together and how to communicate instead of shutting down was huge for us.

Now when conflicts come up instead of giving the 'silent treatment' and being manipulated/controlling we can talk about how we feel and why we feel the way we do."

Alisha

7 Communication Dance
Into-Me-You-See!

Class Topics
- Introduction
- The Goal
- The Styles
- The Levels
- The 'I' Message
- Recap

Communication Problem?
The number one problem in relationships isn't communication, it is the distinct lack of respect during the process of communication!

Introduction
- The Communication Dance is about moving together in a place where we manifest respect.
- Communication comes in many different ways, it should be simple, but it often is not.

Did you just step on my toe in the midst of our communication dance?

7 Communication Dance

Notes

The Goal

- We often dissolve the quality of our communication with the wrong goal.
- Typically, communication has one of two goals: To convince or to agree.
- Either of these goals requires various levels of control of one another in the conversation.
- Control escalates the anxiety and love leaves the scene.
- The **goal** of communication will only succeed to build respect and a safe place for intimacy to grow when the goal is to **understand**.
- Communication should give you a clear understanding of what is going on in both your hearts.
- The practice of identifying, learning and meeting the needs of one another is what will build communication that builds love and trust.

RELATIONSHIP SKILLS SERIES

Into-Me-You-See!

Notes

The Big Secret

- The Big Secret is "*me*"!
- People often hide themselves in relationships because of *fear*.

> You can see into me because I showed you.

- The big prize comes from helping each other unveil ourselves to each other.
- Making myself known requires the practice of intimacy.

    "*Into-me-you-see!*"

- I am going to show you what I need and feel.
- I am going to be vulnerable so I need to feel **safe place** so I can feel **accepted** no matter what.

Defining the Relationship

7 Communication Dance

Notes

We were born to be free
- We are born to be free and feel safe.
- Communication is about creating a *safe place* for people to be themselves and to express their needs to each other.
- The practice of exposing our hearts to each other is extremely vulnerable.
- Fear and defensiveness are poised waiting to manifest because of vulnerability.
- If we learn to experience a safe place while sharing our hearts with each other, then we build *love* and *trust*.
- When we are unable to build this safe place our *needs* go unmet and pain and *anxiety* build in our relationships.

Into-Me-You-See!

- Our need for intimacy does not go away; instead we look for other things to meet our needs.
- Addictions are cycles that emerge in our lives when we cannot reduce the pain and anxiety through loving, intimate connections with people.

Intimacy

- True intimacy **heals** the pain and fear of our disconnections.
- When we practice and experience intimacy as a family our children learn healthy communication tools.
- Generational blessings pass through our everyday examples of respect and honor.

Defining The Relationship

7 Communication Dance

Notes

Unconditional Love
- ***Intimate***, safe communication allows us to experience unconditional love and acceptance.
- This foundation is crucial for you to both share in. No one can make your commitment to creating a safe place but you.
- Early in the relationship you will discover each other's willingness and ability to protect the core value of unconditional love in communication.

"I will love you no matter what we go through!"

Into-Me-You-See!

The Styles

Passive

"You matter and I don't."

- Though seeming to "get along", the Passive is hiding their true feelings and needs and therefore unable to experience unconditional love and acceptance.
- The noble cloak of selflessness is a disguise for scared **selfishness**.
- Passivity is a tool to avoid conflict and to keep from ever being the "bad guy" in the relationship.
- This style creates anxiety in the relationship by keeping the Passive an absolute mystery to their partner. They cannot establish intimacy because they will not let anyone see into their heart.

Defining The Relationship

7 Communication Dance

Notes

Aggressive

"I matter and you don't!"

- Aggressive communicators are accustomed to getting their ***own way*** with clear demands and desires.
- The Aggressive are easy to label as "selfish."
- Their anger is not power, but instead it is how they express their fear and hurt.
- The Aggressive and Passive make a natural connection because they both agree: "My ***needs***, ***feelings*** and ***thoughts***, matter, and yours do not."

RELATIONSHIP SKILLS SERIES

Into-Me-You-See!

Notes

Passive Aggressive

"Oh, YOU matter.... Not!"

- This style incorporates the worst of both styles.
- It is actually the most common among Christian people. We try to hide our negative emotions and needs in a facade of understanding and service.
- The Passive Aggressive communicators do not reveal their true feelings or needs because they are **afraid** it is not valuable, but they are teaming with the rage of feeling **powerless**.
- Sarcasm, veiled threats and empty commitments are common expressions for this communication style.

Defining The Relationship

7 Communication Dance

Assertive

"YOU matter... and so do I!"

- This style requires mutual respect in the communication and relationship.
- Assertive people do not allow others to **pretend** to be powerless nor will they accept the belief that they are **powerless**.
- There are two powerful people in all interactions or relationships or the Assertive sets a limit until both people are powerful again.
- There is no place for blame shifting with an assertive person.

*The goal of our communication **style** is to reduce the **anxiety** of a disagreement or misunderstanding. If our style keeps the focus on self control, respect and protecting the connection, then we will increase our experiences of successful communication with our loved ones.*

The Levels

Cliché:
- The least required for relationship. This is the type of communication we have with absolute *strangers*.

Facts:
- Nothing to argue about here. We simply cite various comments that have a source we can prove if challenged.

Ideas, Opinions & Perspectives:
- This is where is all goes haywire!
- Two people are now showing up in the conversation.
- Differing viewpoints are made manifest.
- These are the thoughts in my head. Here come the disagreements and the anxieties begin to soar.

Into-Me-You-See!

- How you doing?
- Fine. How are you?
- Great!
- Praise the Lord!
- Hallelujah!
- It's supposed to be 85 today.
- Really?
- It was only 73 yesterday.
- I know.
- Cubs are doing great this year: They've won 12 in row.
- There must be a lot of happy Cub fans this year!

sigh

Defining The Relationship

7 Communication Dance

Notes

Feelings:
- This is my experience of the event. It is non-negotiable and real for me. This is my "*heart*".
- If you respond to my heart with your *head*, then I am going to be *hurt*, invalidated and probably feel scared to show it to you again any time soon.

Needs:
- The deepest level of communication resides in what I need as a human being.

  If we get to this level, you will know something powerful about who I am and how you can *strengthen* me. Meeting needs is how we build *trust*.

> I feel afraid when you don't phone and let me know you are going to be late! I need to feel like you are not in danger!!

RELATIONSHIP SKILLS SERIES

Into-Me-You-See!

*For some reason, people have the most difficult time valuing what they **disagree** with or don't understand. This increases the chances of exchanging invalidation messages while **communicating**.*

Learning to allow another person to happen in front of you even though you do not share the same ideas, opinions or perspectives is a communication test many people fail.

Gathering skills to allow people to be themselves, with their own views and experiences helps build the loving, honor relationships we all long for.

If we fail to learn these skills and lessons, we will find ourselves trapped in the shallow levels of clichés and facts. We become afraid to express who we are because of the painful consequences of disagreements or misunderstandings.

Defining The Relationship

7 Communication Dance

Notes

- Therefore, the use of "I" Messages are so helpful:

The 'I' Message

- I feel _____
  (A *feeling*, not a *thought*)
- When _____
  (Describing the *facts* of the event or conversation)
- I need to feel _____
  (A *feeling* and not a *"to do"*)

- Something like this:

  "I feel hurt and invalidated when you don't listen or try to talk me out of what I am feeling. I need to feel understood and valued when I share my heart with you."

  "I feel judged and defensive when you tell me what you think of me. I need to feel protected when you are upset."

  "I feel so loved when you help me with the dishes. I need to feel that. Thanks!"

Into-Me-You-See!

Recap

The Goal
- The _____ of communication will only succeed to build respect and a safe place for intimacy to grow when the goal is to _____.
- The Big Secret
  - The Big Secret is "_____"!
  - People often hide themselves in relationships because of _____.
  - I am going to be vulnerable so I need to feel _____ so I can feel _____ no matter what.
- We were born to be free
  - Communication is about creating a _____ for people to be themselves and to express their needs to each other.
  - If we learn to experience a safe place while sharing our hearts with each other, then we build _____ and _____.
  - When we are unable to build this safe place our _____ go unmet and pain and _____ builds in our relationships.

Defining The Relationship

7 Communication Dance

- Intimacy
  - True intimacy _____ the pain and fear of our disconnections.
- Unconditional Love
  - _____, safe communication allows us to experience unconditional love and acceptance.

The Styles
- Passive *"You matter and I don't."*
  - The noble cloak of selflessness is a disguise for scared _____.
- Aggressive *"I matter and you don't!"*
  - Aggressive communicators are accustomed to getting their _____ with clear demands and desires.
- The Aggressive and Passive make a natural connection because they both agree: "My _____, _____ and _____ matter, and yours do not."
- Passive Aggressive *"Oh, YOU matter.... Not!"*
  - The Passive Aggressive communicators do not reveal their true feelings or needs because they are _____ it is not valuable, but they are teaming with the rage of feeling _____.

Into-Me_You-See!

Assertive *"YOU matter... and so do I!"*
- Assertive people do not allow others to _____ to be powerless nor will they accept the belief that they are _____.

The Levels
- Cliché:
    - This is the type of communication we have with absolute _____.
- Feelings:
    - If you respond to my heart with your _____, then I am going to be _____, invalidated and probably feel scared to show it to you again any time soon.
- Needs:
    - If we get to this level, you will know something powerful about who I am and how you can _____ me. Meeting needs is how we build _____.

The 'I' Message
- I feel... (A _____, not a _____)
- When... (Describing the _____ of the event or conversation)
- I need to feel... (A _____ and not a "_____")

"*Danny taught my husband and me to create a culture of respect with each other. I'll never forget one day I was mad at my husband and I was running my mouth with threats and disrespect. He calmly looked at me and said, "I don't respond to threats, but I do respond to need, what do you need from me?" That one sentence totally diffused the situation and I stood there feeling embarrassed for how I had spoken to him. I know he learned that from Danny and from that day forward I saw my husband in a new light."*

Nicole

RELATIONSHIP SKILLS SERIES

8 Resolving Conflict

Developing a Trust Cycle

Class Topics
- Introduction
- Our Job
- Trust Cycle
- Last Words
- Recap

Trust protects and strengthens

Trust is needed for us to have a strong connection.

When I satisfy the need you express, I build trust in our connection.

Introduction

- One of the goals of resolving conflict is to reduce the *anxiety* in the relationship.

 "There is no fear in love; but perfect love casts out all fear..." 1Jn 4:18

- Seeing things differently from other people doesn't mean we see things better than they do.
- The goal is 2 people in this relationship, two people that are valued and understood!

What do you see?

DEFINING THE RELATIONSHIP

8 Resolving Conflict

Notes

Our Job

The Speaker – DVD Player
- The Speaker must send a *clear* "I" Message.
- "I" Messages are a tremendous help in getting to the needs the speaker has.
- The Speaker can make adjustments to what the Listener hears to better clarify the message and need.

The Listener – The TV
- Remember the goal is to *understand* the message and *needs* of the Speaker.
- Agreement is not the goal!
- Verbal and non-verbal interactions help the Speaker feel *engaged* and *validated*.
- The Listener is not trying to dictate, direct or convince the Speaker.
- They are trying to receive and reflect what the Speaker is saying, feeling and needing.

RELATIONSHIP SKILLS SERIES

Developing a Trust Cycle

Notes

Typical Scenarios – Two DVD players & No Listeners

- As soon as you discover there are no **Listeners**, stop the conversation.
- There will be no successful communication if one of the two important roles is not filled.
- It is usually helpful to allow the one who is most passionate, emotional or upset to be the Speaker first.

DEFINING THE RELATIONSHIP

8 Resolving Conflict

Notes

- If the speaker cannot stay focused on *communicating* what is going inside of them and insists on telling the Listener about the *Listener*, then the Listener must set *limits* with the Speaker.

Something like this:

"I will be glad to listen to you when you can tell me about what is going on inside of you. Right now, I feel attacked and judged. Are you able to talk to me about you or do we need to finish this conversation later?"

I want to share my deepest feelings with you!

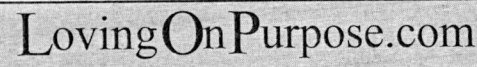

RELATIONSHIP SKILLS SERIES

Developing a Trust Cycle

Trust Cycle

Trust Cycle diagram: Need Awareness → Need Expressed → Respond to Need → Need Satisfied → Comforted (circling around "TRUST CYCLE")

- Trust is needed for us to have a strong **connection**.
- When I satisfy the need you express, I build trust in our connection.

Defining The Relationship

8 Resolving Conflict

Notes

Mistrust Cycle

- Need Awareness
- Need Expressed
- NO Response to Need
- Need NOT Satisfied
- Uncomforted

MISTRUST CYCLE

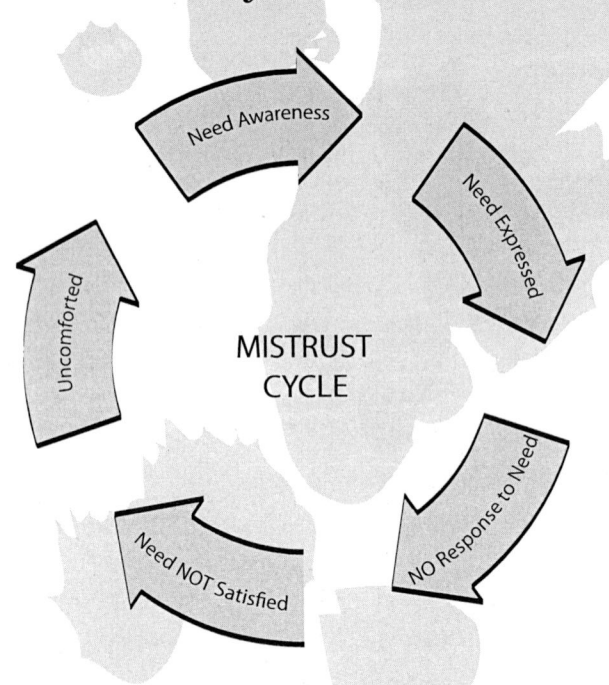

- If we don't have trust, we can't confront each other without increasing the *anxiety* and the need to protect ourselves.

Break the Cycle

*We can break out of this mistrust cycle by learning what other people need, meeting their needs and practicing trust by being **vulnerable** with your needs.*

Developing a Trust Cycle

Last Words

Mercy
- Mercy says I am not your *judge* or your *punisher*. No matter what you do, I don't get to discipline you with punishment based on your decision.
- Mercy triumphs over fear and the result is love.

Use Questions During Conflict
- Questions are a highly effective tool to communicate in a conflict or confrontation.

Defining The Relationship

8 Resolving Conflict

Recap

Introduction
- One of the goals of resolving conflict is to reduce the _____ in the relationship.

Our Job
- The Speaker – DVD Player
  - The Speaker must send a _____ "I" Message.
- The Listener – The TV
  - Remember the goal is to _____ the message and _____ of the Speaker.
  - Verbal and non-verbal interactions help the Speaker feel _____ and _____
- Typical Scenarios – Two DVD players & No Listeners
  - As soon as you discover there is no _____, stop the conversation.
  - If the speaker cannot stay focused on _____ what is going inside of them and insists on telling the Listener about the _____, then the Listener must set _____ with the Speaker.

Developing a Trust Cycle

Trust Cycle
- Trust is needed for us to have a strong _____.

Mistrust Cycle
- If we don't have trust, we can't confront each other without increasing the _____ and the need to protect ourselves.

Break the Cycle
- We can break out of this mistrust cycle by learning what other people need, meeting their needs and practicing trust by being _____ with your needs.

Last Words
- Mercy
  - Mercy says I am not your _____ or your _____. No matter what you do, I don't get to discipline you with punishment based on your decision.

> "*I alone hold the power of choice for who and how much I love another. Nothing someone else does can "make" me not love them anymore. My love is up to me. My love is "ON" toward you, no matter what you say or do. The power of this truth that Danny teaches has ripped the guts out of "lies" that I believed and which made me to feel like someone else could control my love by their behavior or words. This trut has set me free to experience the power to love - on purpose."*
>
> *Kirk*

Defining The Relationship
RELATIONSHIP SKILLS SERIES

9 90/10 Connection
Providing and Protecting Oneness

Class Topics
- Intimacy
- The Difference between Men and Women
  - 90/10 Connection
  - For the Men
  - For the Ladies
- In Closing
- Recap

To Remember
Building a connection is all about your approach to the other person and not about you creating change in the other person.

Notes

Intimacy
- Intimacy is not for wimps!
- Living open toward each other takes great courage, purpose & skill.
- Remember the definition of intimacy?
  - *Into-Me-You-See*
- Can I be free around you, or do I have to hold something back?
- Can I be known and know you fully?
- It is not difficult to cooperate or agree, but it is difficult to connect.

Defining The Relationship

9 90/10 Connection

Notes

- Intimacy creates a unique, connection. It says "I feel the ***best*** about me when I am with ***you***."

Can you handle the truth about my life, because it is so different from who you are.

- When we are connected I feel ***known*** and ***accepted*** and I am able to process my life out loud in front of you.
- When I have to figure out what you need and what you feel, it makes connecting with you 100 times more difficult.

Providing and Protecting Oneness

- The process of reconnecting can be as delicate as letting someone touch your eyeball.
- We have the choice to either *create* true intimacy or contribute to the *illusion* of intimacy.
- Intimacy doesn't just happen and you can't hope to achieve it by changing the other person.
- Intimacy starts with a commitment to *unconditional love*. That is, I can love and thrive in this environment and I will love you no matter what you do.

Defining The Relationship

9 90/10 Connection

Notes

The Difference between Men and Women

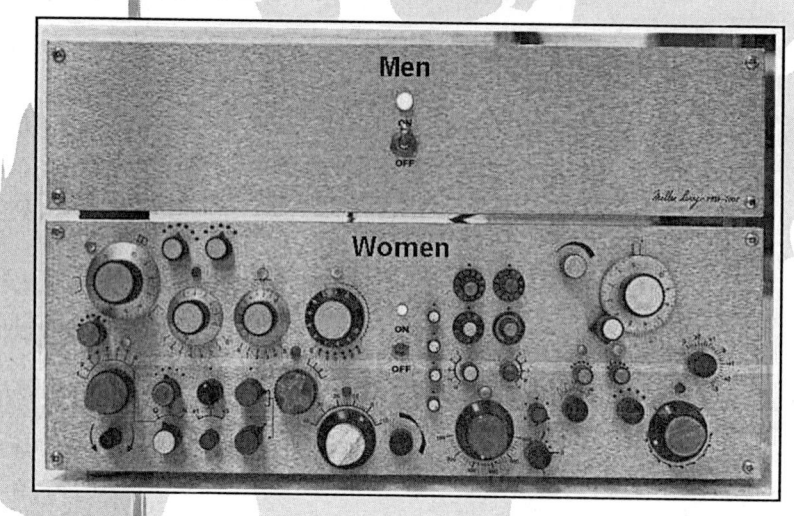

- We are different, because men and women have different motivators built inside of them.
- If you don't understand the differences, this will be a connection breaker for you because we tend not to value what we do not understand.

When it comes to sex, women need a reason and men need a place.

Providing and Protecting Oneness

90/10 Connection

- Men and women are designed to have a different 90%/10% composition.
- Men tend to be motivated by their *sex drives* in a relationship with their lover.
- Women tend to be motivated by their *emotional needs* in a relationship with their lover.
- Each is motivated into their lesser needs by the hope of getting their greater needs fulfilled.
- If we do not learn to communicate our needs and, in turn, learn to *value* what we don't understand, then we end up building the "Mistrust" cycle and the behavior between lovers becomes manipulative and *destructive*.

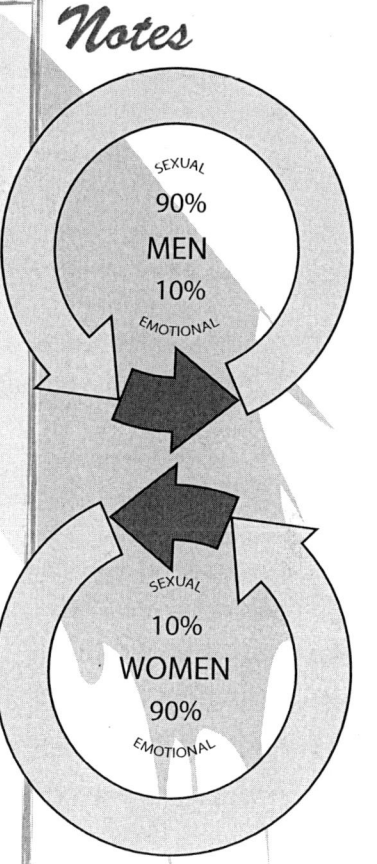

Defining The Relationship

9 90/10 Connection

Notes

For the Men

- Men bear the standard for the love in the relationship flowing at a healthy level. Ephesians 5:25 leads us to this conclusion:

"Husbands, love your wives, just as Christ loved the church and gave himself up for her ..."

- Love her, nourish and cherish her. Pour yourself into <u>your</u> emotional 10% because in doing so she comes alive.

Intimacy is not sex.

- A woman who feels loved, safe and valuable can willingly offer her **vulnerabilities** to her man. Few things make a man feel more like a man than to be in the presence of his lover's **trust**.

- A man will **short-circuit** his own motivations to pursue his wife into her emotions by engaging in **sexual** behaviors without his wife, for example pornography, masturbation.

RELATIONSHIP SKILLS SERIES

Providing and Protecting Oneness

Notes

> "A wise man learns to **engage** his emotional side so he can feed the primary **need** his wife has in the relationship.
>
> A foolish man requires his wife to **sexualize** her emotions so she can have some hope of getting her needs **partially** met in the relationship."

I love surprises. I wonder what you have behind your back?

Defining The Relationship

9 90/10 Connection

Notes

For the Ladies
- The practice of **vulnerability** is a top priority for you to feel emotionally satisfied. Do not allow your heart to become hardened by poor communication. Learn **assertiveness** when it comes to insisting that he value you.
- Taking care of your emotional needs allows you to be present and engage in the sexual relationship with your husband.

"A foolish woman will engage in fantasy and **unhealthy** male attention to stimulate her own **emotions** and short-circuit her motivations to respond to her husband **vulnerably** and sexually."

RELATIONSHIP SKILLS SERIES

Providing and Protecting Oneness

Notes

"A wise woman will **assert** her need for emotional connection by communicating her need to her husband and **avoiding** all sexual manipulation in an effort to feed her own **emotional** needs."

Here Try this, you will love what I have to offer!

9 90/10 Connection

Notes

In Closing:

- The greatest asset a married couple can have together is their heart to heart **connection**. Make this a top priority and your life together will **create** the maturing love that casts out all **fear**.

"In this is love, not that we loved God, but that He loved us and sent His Son to be the (payment) for our sins. Beloved, if God so loved us, we also ought to love one another."

1 John 4:10-11

RELATIONSHIP SKILLS SERIES

Providing and Protecting Oneness

Recap

Introduction

- Intimacy creates a unique, connection. It says "I feel the _____ about me when I am with _____."
- When we are connected I feel _____ and _____ and I am able to process my life out loud in front of you.
- We have the choice to either _____ true intimacy or contribute to the _____ of intimacy.
- Intimacy starts with a commitment to _____. That is, I can love and thrive in this environment and I will love you no matter what you do.

The Difference between Men and Women

- 90/10 Connection
  - Men tend to be motivated by their _____ in a relationship with their lover.
  - Women tend to be motivated by their _____ in a relationship with their lover.
  - If we do not learn to communicate our needs and, in turn, learn to _____

DEFINING THE RELATIONSHIP

9   90/10 Connection

what we don't understand, then we end up building the "Mistrust" cycle and the behavior between lovers becomes manipulative and _____.

- For the Men
  - A woman who feels loved, safe and valuable can willingly offer her _____ to her man. Few things make a man feel like a man than to be in the presence of his lover's _____.
  - A man will _____ his own motivations to pursue his wife into her emotions by engaging in _____ behaviors without his wife, for example pornography, masturbation.
  - "A wise man learns to _____ his emotional side so he can feed the primary _____ his wife has in the relationship.
  - A foolish man requires his wife to _____ her emotions so she can have some hope of getting her needs _____ met in the relationship."
- For the Ladies
  - The practice of _____ is a top prior-

RELATIONSHIP SKILLS SERIES

Providng and Protecting Oneness

ity for you to feel emotionally satisfied. Do not allow your heart to become hardened by poor communication. Learn _____ when it comes to insisting that he value you.

- "A foolish woman will engage in fantasy and _____ male attention to stimulate her own _____ and short-circuit her motivations to respond to her husband _____ and sexually."

- "A wise woman will _____ her need for emotional connection by communicating her need to her husband and _____ all sexual manipulation in an effort to feed her own _____ needs.

In Closing:

- The greatest asset a married couple can have together is their heart to heart _____. Make this a top priority and your life together will _____ the maturing love that casts out all _____.

DEFINING THE RELATIONSHIP

Appendix

Other Resources

When this premarried course is presented at Bethel church in Redding, CA, it includes the following resources referred to on the DVD:
- Prepare/Enrich Asessment
  - www.prepare-enrich.com
- Prosperous Soul: Keys for New Couples by Stephen DeSilva
  - www.bethel.org/store

Bibliography
- Ch.5 refers to the "5 Love Languages" book from Dr. Gary Chapman
  - www.fivelovelanguages.com

Contact Information

Danny Silk - Bethel Church

933 College View Drive

Redding, CA 96003

Tel: (533) 246-6000

Web: LovingOnPurpose.com

RELATIONSHIP SKILLS SERIES

Loving On Purpose
PS 32:8

If you liked this product may we recommend these other popular titles from:
LovingOnPurpose.com

Revolution to Transformation

We live in a day when the experience and practice of church life is in reformation. The core values of a more 'natural' gospel are now replaced with 'supernatural' beliefs and priorities. Our theology, church culture, individual lives and communities will never be the same. We are in the throes of a spiritual and cultural revolution that is leading to a global transformation.

Available in Options:
- CD-Audio
- MP3 Download
- DVD

Powerful & Free: Women in the church

Cultural reformation and revolution lead to freedom and empowerment for all. Somehow, women in the institution of the church have not yet been freed from the "traditions of men." Isn't it a curious trend that we are sending our young people out to impact the most influential leadership roles of our society, but are not teaching our daughters to become apostles? Jesus said it best: "I have come to set the captives free."

Available in Options:
- CD-Audio
- MP3 Download
- DVD

Loving Our Kids On Purpose

Here is a fresh look at the age old role of parenting. Loving Our Kids on Purpose brings the principles of the Kingdom of God and revival into our strategy as parents.

Join the reformation that is transforming a generation! The family is the vehicle for generational revival. Without a different way of training up our children we will not have another result. There is no fear in love, because love casts out all the fear of punishment. Peace!

Available in Options:
- CD-Audio
- MP3 Download
- DVD

Book **COMING SOON!**

LovingOnPurpose.com
© Copyright 2008

Page: 117
Written by: Danny Silk